YES, I AM ENOUGH! THE NEXT LEVEL

Loving, Living, and Sharing Your Enoughness

TANYA WHITE

AWESOME AUTHORS IN ACTION
DELIVERING STAR QUALITY READING SATISFACTION

Yes, I Am Enough!: The Next Level: Loving, Living and Sharing Your Enoughness

Published by Awesome Authors In Action Publishing (AAA Publishing) Louisville, KY

Awesome Authors In Action, Delivering Star Quality Reading Satisfaction

ISBN 978-0-9816847-1-0

Copyright © 2019 by Tanya White.

All rights reserved. No portion of this book may be reproduced, stored in a retrieval system or transmitted in any form or by any means such as electronic, mechanical, photocopy, recording, or any other forms without the prior permission of the publisher except for brief quotations in printed reviews.

Printed in the United States of America

2019-First Edition

DEDICATION

To the Yes, I Am Enough Nation who has been diligent and dedicated in their support of this movement. I am eternally humbled and grateful to walk with you on this journey of Enoughness.

ABOUT THE AUTHOR

Go-Getter. Trailblazer. Visionary. Trendsetter. These are just a few adjectives that describe Tanya White. Whether serving as host and executive producer of her popular Internet radio show, *Real Talk With Tanya White*, speaking to hundreds or coaching individuals and groups, her purpose remains the same: to change people's "No, I Am Not Enough" attitudes into "Yes, I Am Enough" actions.

Tanya is also the author of several other acclaimed books such as *Yes, I Am Enough, You Can't Quit Now, Girl, You Can Win* and *Relationship Reruns,* which are all available for purchase via her website: www.tanyawhite.com. For more information about Tanya, to request a media interview, schedule a coaching session, invite her to be a keynote speaker or to facilitate a workshop at your next event, please call 502-836-9760, visit www.tanyawhite.com or email tanya@tanyawhite.com.

TITLES BY TANYA WHITE

TABLE OF CONTENTS

Introduction 1
Yes, I Am Enough!: How the Movement Began

Chapter 1 7
Six Strategies for Igniting Your Enough Evolution

Chapter 2 20
Embodying Your Enoughness

Chapter 3 35
Loving Your Enoughness

Chapter 4 51
Living Your Enoughness

Chapter 5 62
Sharing Your Enoughness

Closing 78
Yes, I Am Enough!: From the Next Level to Being Magnetically Phenomenal

References 85

INTRODUCTION

YES, I AM ENOUGH!
How the Movement Began

"We came into the world saturated in the fullness of our God-given enoughness. He made certain that we were specially designed with footprints of excellence, lacking nothing." — Tanya White

YES, I AM ENOUGH! I would have never expected that these four words would have become the daily declaration of men and women around the world. I wrote this book from my heart and life's experience. The Lord told me not to just have a book release event with *Yes, I Am Enough*, but to have a spiritual empowerment conference for women. I obeyed, even though I did not know why He wanted me to do this.

On April 7, 2018, the *Yes, I Am Enough: Mind, Body and Soul Spiritual Empowerment Extravaganza* happened. Though my expectation was to have only about 50 women to attend, over 100 men and women attended. To date, I continue to receive testimonies of how that conference shifted people's lives for the better. Releasing the first *Yes, I Am Enough* book was a supernatural demonstration of God's Ephesians 3:20 declaration.

YES, I AM ENOUGH was a life epiphany that occurred during one of the most stressful and stretching times of my life. After being engulfed in an unexpected Saul and David situation, I was at my wit's end. I was living in my own version of Psalm 142:1-7.

"God, I'm crying out to you! I lift up my voice boldly to beg for your mercy. I spill out my heart to you and tell you all my troubles. For when I was desperate, overwhelmed, and about to give up, you were the only one there to help. You gave me a way of escape from the hidden traps of my enemies. I look to my left and right to see if there is anyone who will help, but there's no one who takes notice of me. I have no hope of escape, and no one cares whether I live or die. So, I cried out to you, Lord, my only hiding place. You're all I have, my only hope in this life, my last chance for help. Please listen to my heart's cry, for I am low and in desperate need of you! Rescue me from all those who persecute me, for I am no match for them. Bring me out of this dungeon so I can declare your praise! And all your godly lovers will celebrate all the wonderful things you've done for me!" Psalm 142:1-7 (The Passion Translation)

Why was I allowing the opinion of a small group of people to drive me to a spirit of defeat when their only connection to me was to band together to break me down? Why did

Introduction

I believe the report of a manipulative, messy, and insecure leader and start asking myself all of those common enough questions? I had allowed the pessimistic opinions and actions of a small percentage of people to paralyze a large percentage of my life.

My Saul and David situation had me depressed. I was discouraged. I felt defeated. I stopped living with purpose and confidence. My heart was breaking. My soul had a hole in it. My sinister Saul was strategically abusing his influence over me to ruin the life that I prayed and prepared for. No matter how much I tried to convince my Saul that I had not wronged him neither did I have anything against him, the false attacks intensified.

I was asking myself a plethora of "Am I Enough?" questions. All of that had compelled me to question everything I knew about myself. Until one day, I was in my room, crying desperately. Then, something quickened in me to yell out as though I was at a New Edition concert, trying to get their attention—"**YES, I AM ENOUGH!**"

On April 7, 2018, my struggle was unleashed, creating a haven of saving grace for over 100 women and men who attended my first ever *Yes, I Am Enough* Book Release/Empowerment Conference. The Yes, I Am Enough Nation was formed. T-shirts, books, testimonies with the words: **YES, I AM ENOUGH** stirred people up.

Since my first *Yes, I Am Enough* book release, soul wounds have been healed. Hearts have been mended. Destinies have finally been manifested. There is power in these four words that will continue to shake men, women, children and me as well.

How to Utilize Yes, I Am Enough, the Next Level

In this book, I move from just sharing information to encouraging you with implementation. Each chapter focuses on strategies that will take you to the next level. Also, I conclude every chapter with a prayer of affirmation. Finally, there are activities to prompt self-reflection and strategic planning.

It is my prayer that as you read this book, you literally feel the presence of God's confirmation. I hope to inspire you to willingly apply the strategies. Recite the prayer affirmation out loud. Complete the end-of-chapter activities. Understand that next-level living entails next-level commitment.

This will be a journey like none other. Are you ready to go higher? Are you ready to dig deeper? Are you ready to walk in the reality of your dreams? Well, it all begins with you making up your mind to go to the next level before you live at the next level.

Become an active and participatory reader with this book. Embody your enoughness. Love your enoughness. Live and share your enoughness. If at any point throughout this book thoughts of "No, I Am Not Enough" start to stalk your mind, just yell out like you are at your favorite concert, **"YES, I AM ENOUGH"** because you truly are!

Introduction

Let us recite the first prayer affirmation:

*"Lord, as I begin my next-level journey, help me to eliminate thoughts that will keep me stuck. Purge my heart from the hurts and harm that have kept me bleeding emotionally, mentally and spiritually. I release the years of pain, discouragement and defeat. I open my heart to what You want to speak to me. Lord, I am holding on to Your word in 2 Corinthians 4:7-9 'But we have this treasure in jars of clay to show that this all-surpassing power is from God and not from us.' I am hard pressed on every side, but not crushed; perplexed, but not in despair; persecuted, but not abandoned; struck down, but not destroyed. Despite all that I have been through, I will continuously remind myself that **YES, I AM ENOUGH** because I am created in Your wonderful image. God, I am ready to go to the next level. In the name of Jesus, take me there. Amen."*

NEXT-LEVEL IMPLEMENTATION

In the space below, identify three to five things you hope to glean from this book. Then, write yourself a brief commitment pledge to the **YES, I AM ENOUGH** experience.

_____

_____

_____

_____

_____

_____

_____

_____

_____

_____

_____

_____

_____

_____

CHAPTER 1

Six Strategies for Igniting Your Enough Evolution

"Life is all about evolution. What looks like a mistake to others has been a milestone in my life. Even if people have betrayed me, even if my heart was broken, even if people misunderstood or judged me, I have learned from these incidents. We are human and we make mistakes, but learning from them is what makes the difference."
— Amisha Patel

If you are the same person you were six months ago, one year ago, three years ago and, God forbid, ten years ago, you are not living life. You are simply existing. To truly live life at the next level of evolution requires discipline and determination.

Evolution is much deeper than the concept of changing. The word "change" means *to make or become different; the act or instance of making or becoming different.* On the contrary, "evolution" is a *gradual development from simple to a more complex form; the cumulative inherited change in a population of organisms through time leading to the appearance of new forms.*

When I think of change, it is a quick movement that does not require much thought. For example, when I am getting dressed for an event, I usually change jewelry, shoes and sometimes complete outfits before I leave. Why? Because I am trying to feel satisfied with a certain look.

The swift changes I make when going to a one-time event is rooted in a superficial vision. Upon a quick glance at the outfits, I want to look presentable and beautiful to onlookers. These onlookers, for the most part, will be people I will never see again. However, I want to give them a memorable impression. That is how I perceive the concept of change. Change is quick and can be superficial at times.

Yet, evolution requires precision, preparation, and power. Evolution is much like when I am writing a book. I abandon the craving to have a superficial response from people I may never encounter again. I literally pour out everything I have throughout the pages of my books. In order to properly pour, I must do more.

As opposed to when I am attending an event and change in anxiousness, in order to achieve a particular appearance, writing is an evolution for me. I want my readers to experience the authentic essence of who I am and what God is trying to say through me. That compels me to evolve instead of change.

Change is easy. Change is thoughtless. Change can be a defense mechanism for avoiding examining the core system of your living.

Six Strategies for Igniting Your Enough Evolution

Yet, evolution is complex. Evolution prompts you to have a profound insight into who you are, what you are equipped to do and how you will get there. You cannot be more concerned with how you look than the character of who you are when you are focused on evolving into your enoughness.

Evolution demands an inner reflection of the totality of who you are. However, in that self-critique, you still have a basic understanding that you are enough. It requires strategy and support systems of substance. When you truly want to evolve into loving, living and sharing that you are God-enough, you must do things that make you uncomfortable.

In the remaining sections of this chapter, I will discuss the six strategies for igniting your enough evolution. Implementing these strategies create feelings of uneasiness. But when you press your way through, you will be liberated like never been before.

Excavate Your Mindsets, Motives, and Movements That Are Keeping You Stuck In A Rut

Mindsets, motives and movements will keep you as a castaway on the island of "I'm Not Enough." You must excavate or dig up all those things that are contaminating the image of God. Remember, He created us to be a reflection of Himself.

First, our mindsets need to imitate the mind of Christ. Knowing that we are enough is not an arrogant thought that we are equal to God because we are created in His image. On the contrary, it is heavenly confidence that humbles us to have righteous motives and respectful actions.

Philippians 2:5-8 explains, *"Let this mind be in you, which was also in Christ Jesus, Who, being in the form of God, thought it not robbery to be equal with God: But made himself of no reputation, and took upon him the form of a servant, and was made in the likeness of men: And being found in fashion as a man, he humbled himself, and became obedient unto death, even the death of the cross."*

Going to the next level will require you to forego your cravings to have a famous reputation. Regardless of your title, you must have the mind of a servant toward **everyone at all times.** As you develop the mind of a servant, your motives will become free of hidden agendas, selfish gain and hustling people to obtain what you want.

With the mindset of a servant, coupled with the motives of the Savior, it is inevitable that your movements will obey what God expects. Even when the Lord orchestrates your movements to places and situations that you do not understand, you will still obey. Elevating your enoughness to the next level entails excavating.

Nurture the Godsent Connections in Your Life

Every connection that comes into your life is not a Godsent connection, although it was God allowed. When you are genuinely in relationships with people, you can do a connection check to determine if they are truly of the Lord. Godsent connections encourage you to evolve. They are not afraid of speaking truth in love. They would rather have a healthy conflict by speaking truth than being a fake connection that kills you softly.

True God connections are relationships like David and Jonathan in the Bible. Their divine friendship demonstrated loyalty of future purpose instead of loyalty to the family patriarch who was jealous, insecure and vengeful. Jonathan knew how to release his dysfunctional family ties to pour into his friend, David, who was anointed the future king, a position that should have been Jonathan's inheritance.

Godsent connections are like Mary and Elizabeth. Mary, who was in an unusual situation that had her walking in unknown territory because she was chosen to birth a world changer, knew Elizabeth had her own battle that was stressing her out. So, a pregnant Mary traveled to be with her cousin. Mary's presence made the baby in Elizabeth, which had not moved in months, leap at the mere sound of her voice. Now that is a divine connection!

We are living in a society that would much rather have fake than authentic relationships. That is why people disconnect from those anointed to make their inner baby leap. They choose to stay connected to people who caress their egos but do not ignite an inner movement in their lives. True God connections give you a surge of **P.O.W.E.R.** to prompt you to evolve into your enoughness.

Your **P.O.W.E.R.** comes as a result of your Godsent connections that are:

Pure—There should be no poisonous contamination. The motives are pure. The boundaries are clear. Nothing clouds this connection.

Optimistic—Connections that are always pessimistic, create problems. Optimism opens you to more opportunities.

Win-Win—Power connections always find healthy compromises to birth an atmosphere of hope and a win-win situation. People who always want to have their way and throw covert and overt tantrums drain you.

Evolving—It blows my mind when people brag on how long they have been friends and there has been no evolution to advance them individually or collectively. If you are in relationships that are not evolving, it is because you do not know your enoughness.

Reciprocal—One-sided relationships deplete you. Connections of power are established on the principle of reciprocity. Reciprocity in a relationship is the practice of exchanging ideas, words of encouragement and advice with others for mutual benefits. When you are void of reciprocity in a relationship, your enoughisms will escalate.

You will always wonder "Am I good enough? Am I loveable enough? Am I worthy enough?" Yes, you are enough. You are just connected to someone who is transferring their "NO, I'M NOT ENOUGH!" spirit in the relationship because there is no reciprocity. When your connections become powerless, give that relationship the necessary free gift of your goodbye.

Overcome the Trauma and Pain of Your Past

It is a fact of life that unhealed childhood trauma leads to adulthood drama. Operating out of the pain of your past paralyzes your future. Sadly, many individuals believe that they have been delivered from the trauma and pain of their past, but that is a pseudo-deliverance.

Pseudo-deliverance is when you have the illusion that you have moved on, but in reality, the players in your painful situation have moved out of your physical proximity. That is not healing. That is masking your hurt.

True healing comes from doing an emotional autopsy of the situation. It entails, processing the what, when, why, and how of what hurt you. Authentic deliverance is when you can say, from the gut of your soul, that "Whatever state I find myself in, I have learned how to be content. I know that all things are working together for my good because I love God."

Authentic deliverance is when you are truly focused on fixing what is breaking you in life. It is working through the trauma to transform it into triumph. Genuine healing is viewing life as Amisha Patel explained in her statement below about the evolution:

"Life is all about evolution. What looks like a mistake to others has been a milestone in my life. Even if people have betrayed me, even if my heart was broken, even if

people misunderstood or judged me, I have learned from these incidents. We are human and we make mistakes, but learning from them is what makes the difference."

Unleash the True You

When you are not living in the power of knowing that you are enough, you will begin to put on masks. Masks of position and title. Masks of success. Masks of being in love. Masks of approval addiction. Masks of power, promiscuity, pride, and perfectionism. When you are oblivious to your actual worth, you will consistently put on the masks of performing instead of producing the fruit that God planted in you.

However, did you know that when you wear a mask, people can see through it? Consider a costume mask with slits that are strategically positioned. The slits allow people to have a glimpse of identifiable parts to detect who is behind the mask.

In the same manner, there are identifiable slits in the mask that you wear. For instance, behind the mask of perfectionism is a small opening that people can see that you are really void of knowing your worth. Worth does not come from what you do or how you do it. Worth is a God-given trait that can never be taken away. You were created in His image. That alone makes you worth more than anything.

If you are wearing this mask, as well as other masks, take them off. Unleash the true you. Love yourself, flaws and all.

Six Strategies for Igniting Your Enough Evolution

Living in the truth of who you are will free you to evolve into your enoughness.

Set Goals and Implement the Goals That You Set

Where there is no vision or goals, you will walk in constant feelings of inadequacy and incompetence. When you know you are born and built God-enough, you are not afraid to set goals. Not only will you set goals according to your divine promise, but you will also implement the goals you set without procrastination.

As a consultant, coach, and mentor, I can immediately predict the level of success that a client/mentee will have. People who are easily distracted really do not believe in their enoughness. People who set unrealistic goals with no strategy are not walking in enoughness. The biggest deceptive illusion that Christians use is the infamous "God told me to do this."

Let me divinely disrupt that deceptive façade. My God is a God of strategy, preparation, and goal-setting. The type of goal-setting that is not birthed out of an egotistical need or a selfish craving for attention. The Lord does things with a vision and purpose of providing a universal blessing.

After my first *Yes, I Am Enough* conference, someone told me that God wanted them to put on a conference that year and four hundred people would attend it. Now, first of all, I know that God can do anything. But He does things well and not out of vainglory. This person's desire to host a conference was out of vanity.

Why do I say this? First of all, this person did not even have an audience that they were nurturing with their God-given message at the time. They admitted that the reason they were not further along in life was that they were easily distracted and that was the most honest self-confession they ever made during our connection.

Next, they had no definite strategy of orchestrating the conference. They wanted to have the event within a four-month time frame. They suffered from a severe case of the "I don't know yet."

Me:	Well, where are you going to have it?
Them:	I don't know yet.
Me:	What is your purpose and theme of the conference?
Them:	I don't know yet.
Me:	Are you going to have speakers, classes—what is the format?
Them:	I don't know yet.
Me:	What is your budget for the conference?
Them:	I don't know yet. I just know God told me to put on a conference and four hundred people will be there.

Vainglory. They were all talk and directionless action. That conversation involved tons of self-gratifying objectives.

They had no definite strategy of execution. No goals. No vision. Just vanity. God may not reveal all the details when He instructs us. However, He will definitely reveal the purpose of what He wants us to do. When the Lord sees that you are competing for His glory, He will shut down everything that you are trying to accomplish.

Seek God for your goals. Pray to Him to help you implement the goals. Next-level living requires next level goal-setting. Next-level living also needs next-level strategic and well-thought-out goal-implementation.

Have a Designated Time to Care for Yourself

Evolving into your enoughness will prompt you to schedule time for rest. Remember, evolution is a process of development. The process requires a great deal of physical, emotional, and spiritual energy. Exercise your divine right to rest.

Genesis 2:2 shows us that the Lord even took care of Himself. *"By the seventh day God had finished the work He had been doing; so on the seventh day He rested from all his work."* The Lord was so secure in who He was and what He was working for, that rest was a part of His divine schedule. People who believe that being busy demonstrates productivity or creates an elevated status of holiness are truly trapped in deception.

When you are advancing your enoughness, you embrace taking a break to rest. God rested. You need to rest. Take the time to care for yourself before you find yourself hospitalized, with a staff of medical professionals taking care of you.

I close this chapter with the "Yes, I Am Enough to Live at the Next Level" prayer affirmation.

"Heavenly Father, You are everything to me. You are my Savior, my Protector, my Waymaker, my Peace, my Joy, my Advocate, my Healer, my Deliverer, my Redeemer, my Everything. It is my heart's desire not to stay stagnant. I want to evolve in my divine enoughness. **YES, I AM ENOUGH TO LIVE AT THE NEXT LEVEL!**

"It is your desire that I move to the next level of believing that I am worthy, capable, adequate, and simply enough. Your word says in 2 Corinthians 3:18, 'But we all, with unveiled face, beholding as in a mirror the glory of the Lord, are being transformed into the same image from glory to glory, just as by the Spirit of the Lord.' **SO, YES, I AM ENOUGH TO LIVE AT MY NEXT LEVEL!**

"God, you endowed me with power. I should not fear my power. I should not allow other people to drain, diminish, or deaden my power. Lord, I repent of willingly creating a life of powerlessness because of fear, staying connected to unequally yoked relationships, and focusing on the storms of life. 2 Timothy 1:7 declares that You did not give me the spirit of fear but of power, love, and a sound mind. And because of that power, love, and sound mind, I will remember that **YES, I AM ENOUGH TO LIVE AT MY NEXT LEVEL!** In Jesus' name. Amen."

Six Strategies for Igniting Your Enough Evolution

NEXT-LEVEL IMPLEMENTATION

It is time to do a thorough **P.O.W.E.R.** connection check. In the table below, list four people you spend the majority of time with from your family, friends, workplace and/or church. You are going to determine if these connections are birthing power or draining you of your power.

If they are giving you power, then determine how you will nurture that connection to the next level. However, if you discover that it is draining you, do not hesitate to start wrapping your beautiful gift of goodbye without apology, shame, or wavering. **BE HONEST and DETAILED!**

	Connection #1 Name:	Connection #2 Name:	Connection #3 Name:	Connection #4 Name:
Is the connection PURE?				
Is the connection OPTIMISTIC?				
Does the connection encourage WIN-WIN encounters?				
Is the connection EVOLVING?				
Is the connection RECIPROCAL?				

CHAPTER 2

Embodying Your Enoughness

Don't explain your philosophy. Embody it."
— *Epictetus*

Embody: (verb)—be an expression of or give a tangible or visible form to (an idea, quality, or feeling).

The first step of next-level living in your enoughness is to embody the totality of it. As the above definition states, when you embody something, there will be tangible results. Yet, sadly, society today has embodied a poisonous ideology that is producing tangible results that are extremely superficial. We are embracing a deadly "ism" that is destroying our productivity and forward movement. We are suffering from global and international pseudoism.

What is pseudoism? It is the continuous inclination to live and love what is false and artificial. We suffer from pseudoism in our government leadership. We are being divided by pseudoism in our community leadership. Even in our churches, God's children are dying spiritually, emotionally, and, yes, even physically from the increase in suicide and homicide due to the superficial, deceptive, and demonic pseudoism leadership.

What is real has become offensive. Truth is abruptly rejected. People who operate under pseudoism have mastered persuading people to view the authentic as artificial. Even our current leader of the United States, the 45th President has ignited a war on the media especially, calling people and organizations fake who speak against his falsities.

However, the 45th Commander-In-Chief is not the only person operating in this manner. We are in the age of where people are working themselves to death to save for plastic surgery instead of a prosperous future. As a result, this craving for the artificial has birthed an unexpected emotional and mental tsunami. This unhealthy thirst to masquerade as something you were not created to be, has deadly consequences.

The Origination of the Pseudo Phenomena

Years ago, the marvelous Mark Twain made adopting a pseudonym an innovative paradigm in the literary arena. Research explains that he was born Samuel Langhorne Clemens on November 30, 1835, in Missouri. Life brought him many struggles from the death of siblings to the death of his father. Clemens dropped out of school in the fifth grade.

He then became a printer's apprentice and eventually wrote articles for the newspaper.

Although it was apparent that writing was a gifted passion for Clemens, nonetheless, a boy growing up by the Mississippi River had one dream and one dream only. That ambition of future bliss entailed becoming a steamboat pilot. To obtain this grandiose and prestigious position brought Clemens not only personal notoriety but a new name—Mark Twain.

Now, the newly stamped Twain renamed himself to resemble the manifestation of achieving his dream. Unlike most pseudonyms, Clemens pen name had deep meaning and reflected what he was purposed to pour out in his writings. The website www.thoughtco.com writes that the name "Mark Twain" was a steamboat term. The term means the *stage and condition of the river, being accurate and valuable; and containing no poison.*

Unlike Twain's meaningful name change, many people have aimlessly gravitated toward creating a false persona. The abundant life that Jesus said that He came to give us has been traded in for artificial self-perception, fake relationships, deceptive visions, and surrounding ourselves with demonic voices that speak to us out of emotion instead of the authentic assignment of God. This is partly because they have either denied, been deceived, or dismissed their God-given enoughness. When you have no genuine knowledge of who you are, you will always think that you lack something.

The "No, I'm Not Enough" Life Formula

There is an unconscious life formula that people operate in when they have made pseudoism a way of life. Pseudoism becomes the justification for internalizing the misnomer "Fake it until you make it" philosophy. But when the making it never manifests, the faking it births a life of living behind masks.

The "No, I'm Not Enough" formula is:
- **Insecurity** (anxiety about yourself and lacking confidence; not feeling protected)
- **Inferiority** (believing that you are less than or of lower position)
- <u>**Inadequacy** (thinking that you have an insufficient purpose; incapable)</u> = **ILLUSIONS OF "NO, I'M NOT ENOUGH!"**

The deliberate acceptance of living a life that is phony can be traced to the seeds of insecurity, inferiority, and inadequacy. Those seeds germinate. Then, the unwanted branches of illusions grow into a humongous tree called "No, I'm Not Enough." As a sad result, these illusions eventually compel people to ignore their divine origination to embody a personal imitation. Again, I say, when you have no genuine knowledge of who you are, you will always think you lack something.

In her book, *Taking Off the Mask*, Brenda Richmond-Davis wrote that *"the word illusion means a false idea or conception; an unreal or misleading appearance or image. An illusion is basically a lie."* If you agree with the illusions that your insecurity, inferiority, and inadequacy have led you to internalize, then you are living a lie. Lies are of the devil. So, therefore, if you choose to live a life engulfed with lies because you operate under the "No, I'm Not Enough" formula, then you are a child of your true father—the devil.

I did not call you a devil-child, Jesus did. In John 8:43-44, He declares, *"Why can't you understand what I am saying? It is because you are prevented from doing so! For you are the children of your father the devil and you love to do the evil things he does. He was a murderer from the beginning and a hater of truth—there is not an iota of truth in him. When he lies, it is perfectly normal; for he is the father of liars,"* (The Living Bible Translation). When you refuse to understand the depth, width, and breadth of who you were created to be and who God says you are, there is an unstable force that prevents you from it. That force is the devil—the father of lies.

S.T.E.A.M. Your Way to Destroying Your "No, I'm Not Enough" Illusions

In order to embody your enoughness, you first must acknowledge that you are flowing in the "No, I'm Not Enough" life formula that has snatched your innate power. The first step that Alcoholics Anonymous recommends for the road to recovery is to admit you are powerlessness because of your addiction. If you have this book in your hand, trust me, you have been or are currently a "No, I'm Not Enough" addict.

But the good news is that you can become your own steamboat pilot like the great Mark Twain. Remember, his name literally means *"a stage and condition…of being accurate and valuable; containing no poison."* Recognizing that you having been living an illusion that has contaminated your thinking, living, and loving will desperately require you to do something drastic. Author Brenda Richmond-Davis pinned the term **illusion annihilation.** She wrote in her book, *Taking Off the Mask,* that **illusion annihilation** is *"constantly getting rid of, or destroying the lies that we believe."*

In order to truly annihilate the illusions so you can embody your God-given enoughness, you must unleash an anointed **S.T.E.A.M.** This will allow you to position yourself on the pathway to your "Yes, I Am Enough" recovery.

How do you do that? Well, it is imperative that you:

- **S**ay **Who God Says You Are with Clarity!**—No longer will you believe the lies about who you are not. Stand boldly in who God says you are. Go to His Word that says you are fearfully and wonderfully made. You are the head and not the tail. You have dominion, power, and authority. You are a force of unstoppable supernatural significance.

    Anything or anyone who tries to convince you of something contrary to who God says you are is of the devil. Like Jesus did Peter, you need to rebuke people who speak words that are opposite of who you were divinely created to be. So, speak God's Word with clarity and the devil will flee immediately. You are ENOUGH in the eyes of God.

- **Think About What God Says Consistently!**—Our thinking is primarily developed by what and who we surround our lives with. My daddy used to tell us growing up, *"If you hang around dummies, then you will eventually become a dummy yourself."* So, in the same vein of my daddy, Joe White, Sr., I will tell you that if you want to start thinking differently, then surround your atmosphere with the difference you seek. If you want to consistently think you are enough, insulate your circle, especially your inner circle, with people who have clarity about knowing they are enough, too.

What we meditate on and who we mingle with will determine what we manifest. King David kicked off the prolific book of Psalm 1:1-3 of the New Living Translation, with these attitude shifting words of truth of what happens when you think about what the Word of God says. *"Oh, the joys of those who do not, follow the advice of the wicked, or stand around with sinners, or join in with mockers. But they delight in the law of the* LORD, MEDITATING ON IT DAY AND NIGHT. *They are like trees planted along the riverbank, bearing fruit each season. Their leaves never wither, and they prosper in all they do."*

Let this scripture be your daily atmosphere shifter. When you are feeling the itch to indulge in a lethal dose of "No, I'm Not Enough" thinking, check what and who has been in your atmosphere. Be courageous enough to say goodbye when they have become steam engines of stinking thinking in your life.

- **Evolve into the Prosperous Person God Wants You to Become Continuously!**—Reject all the miseducation and error that you may have been taught that the Lord is not concerned with us being prosperous or having a successful future. That is an illusion that needs to be annihilated and eliminated from your thinking. Before the first man was even thought of, God had prosperity in the plans of man. Reread Genesis 1:28-29.

  In addition, Jeremiah 29:11 declares, *"I alone know the plans I have for you, plans to bring you prosperity and not disaster, plans to bring about the future you hope for."* Philippians 4:19 promises, *"But my God shall supply all your need according to his riches in glory by Christ Jesus."* Deuteronomy 28:13 declares, *"If you listen to these commands of the LORD YOUR GOD THAT I AM GIVING YOU TODAY, AND IF YOU CAREFULLY OBEY THEM, THE LORD*

WILL MAKE YOU THE HEAD AND NOT THE TAIL, AND YOU WILL ALWAYS BE ON TOP AND NEVER AT THE BOTTOM."

The Bible is laced with the philosophy that the Lord desires for you to be prosperous in all things. Stop limiting prosperity to only money. Our Father has a heart of holistic prosperity. Yes, you are enough to evolve into the prosperous person He has predestined you to be.

- **Accept That You Are Enough Courageously!**—You can say that you are enough. You can even have other people declare that you are enough. But if you do not accept the truth that you lack nothing in God, then what you speak is in vain. Acceptance is key to embodying your enoughness.

    Have you ever given someone a genuine compliment and they reject it? How did that make you feel? Better yet, did you feel sorry for them because they did not feel worthy enough to receive positive words about how you saw them?

    Imagine how the Lord feels when you reject your heavenly gift of enoughness. Accept that you are enough with humble courage. And do not apologize or minimize the lavish and expensive gift that God gave you.

NEXT-LEVEL IMPLEMENTATION

In this chapter, I discussed the "No, I'm Not Enough" formula below:
- **Insecurity (anxiety about yourself and lacking confidence; not feeling protected)**
- **Inferiority (believing that you are less than or of lower position)**
- <u>**Inadequacy (thinking that you have an insufficient purpose; incapable)**</u> = ILLUSIONS OF "NO, I'M NOT ENOUGH!"
   1) In the space provided, input the information from your life to complete the formula. Look at my example and then repeat with your information.

Tanya's "No, I'm Not Enough" formula:
- **Insecurity**—I have anxiety about making decisions that advance my life/purpose, but cause me to leave friends, organizations, and situations that I have become comfortable with, even though I may be stuck and stagnant. I feel emotionally unprotected because I know my leaving will cause tension with others.
- **Inferiority**—The above insecurity births feelings of inferiority when I finally make the transition. I feel rejected by the friends, organizations,

and situations that I left. In the same manner, I feel less than in new environments because I still battle real or perceived feelings of rejection.

- **Inadequacy**—As my feelings of insecurity and inferiority work in demonic synchronicity, I start to shrink in the background. For example, in new organizations, I will tend to hide my gifts and talents because they may have been ignored, dismissed or mocked in other situations. I begin to think that my purpose and talents are not effective or sufficient.

ILLUSIONS OF "NO, I'M NOT ENOUGH!"

I am not loveable enough, flexible enough, patient enough, loyal enough, competent enough, compassionate enough, or understanding enough. But all this is a lie! **YES, I AM ENOUGH!**

Embodying Your Enoughness

Now, you can complete your own formula. Be honest and dig deep.

My Insecurity: _____
_____
_____
_____
_____

My Inferiority: _____
_____
_____
_____
_____

My Inadequacy: _____
_____
_____
_____
_____

My Illusions of "NO, I'M NOT ENOUGH!": _____

_____

_____

_____

_____

_____

2) Now that you have the formula, identify three to five ways you will combat and not internalize your insecurity, inferiority, and inadequacy. _____

_____

_____

_____

_____

_____

_____

_____

_____

_____

_____

CHAPTER 3

Loving Your Enoughness

"Loving yourself isn't vanity. It is sanity."
— André Cide

Love is a term that is totally misused, abused, and manipulated. Our biggest mistake is only viewing love in one dimension. Oftentimes, love is only seen as a noun. But to embrace the totality of the concept of love, we must view it simultaneously as an attitude (noun) and as an action (verb).

In friendships, love is limited to current feelings about the relationship instead of being based on a covenant vow.

In romantic relationships, love has been diminished to a lustful feeling of the performance in sexual intercourse. Oh, how this thing called love has been twisted and tainted.

But the most important attribute of God is that He is love. And if we want to love the right way, we must look to the Lord. The Lord is *love* the noun and *love* the verb. When we comprehend the complete scope of what love is then we will know that we are enough. As we learn to love the way God loves, then we will first love ourselves properly and then others.

The 7 Types of Love

Loving your enoughness at another level must entail you recognizing that there are various types of love. Seven types to be exact. According to the article by Neel Burton, M.D. on www.psychologytoday.com entitled "These Are the 7 Types of Love," the categories of love are:

1. *Agape:* This is the nature of God. It is a universal, unending, unselfish, and unconditional love. When you love this way, forgiveness, mercy, patience, and being open to reconciliation are essential to implement.

2. *Eros:* This is the type of love that people first think about. It is the most superficial love because it is limited to sexual or passionate physical love. Next-level enoughness expands your view of love outside of just being this feeling of goosebumps, physical stimulation, and sexual pleasure.

3. **Philia:** This is an authentic love in a friendship. There is mutual benefit, companionship, goodwill, dependability, and trust.

4. **Storge:** This is the love you have for your family. It is born out of familiarity and dependency that does not get hung up on personal successes or shortfalls. Family love is unconditional and free of ulterior motives.

5. **Ludus:** This article states that this is *"playful or uncommitted love. It can involve activities such as teasing and dancing, or more overt flirting, seducing, and conjugating. The focus is on fun, and sometimes also on conquest, with no strings attached. Ludus relationships are casual, undemanding, and uncomplicated."*

6. **Pragma:** The article explains that pragma love, "*is a kind of practical love founded on reason or duty and one's longer-term interests. Sexual attraction takes a back seat in favour of personal qualities and compatibilities, shared goals, and making it work.*"

7. **Philautia:** This is self-love. Self-love can be either healthy or unhealthy. However, a healthy philautia love is equivalent to saying "Yes, I Am Enough!" Your

level of philautia love determines how you think, feel, and act in relation to yourself, to others, and to the world.

The 5 Languages of Loving Your Enoughness

In 1995, like millions of other readers, I was immediately transformed by the 5 Languages of Love concept based on Gary Chapman's national bestselling book of the same name. The primary focus of the project was to teach married couples how to genuinely express heartfelt commitment to each other. This commitment would be demonstrated in a language that the other person could clearly understand and embrace.

Love. It is a simple yet complex concept. It is simple because it should be effortless. Complex because in order to truly love from a foundation of the agape type of God love, we need to put on the mind of love. Yes, we need to think about how to love people the way they need to be loved instead of how we want and need to be loved. And that was what catapulted Chapman's theory into the next-level stratosphere that revolutionized how this world loves not only their spouses but everyone.

As I reflected on the 5 languages of love, I discovered that walking in the next level of being confident, secure, and feeling adequate creates languages of enoughness. Much like Chapman's theory, better communication of your enoughness can be accomplished through a consistent demonstration in an active language that people can understand.

Loving Your Enoughness

There were many more languages of enoughness on my first list. However, I narrowed them down to five, which include:

- ➢ **Acts of accountability:** An excellent definition of accountability is found via www.businessdictionary.com. It defines accountability as *the obligation of an individual or organization to* ***account*** *for its activities,* ***accept*** *responsibility for them, and to* ***disclose*** *the results in a* ***transparent manner****.* Insecure people reject being accountable to others because they have a distorted view that accountability is a method of manipulative control. On the contrary, it is not about control but a blessed assurance that you stay on track to being triumphant every day.

    In his www.forbes.com article, Joseph Folkman revealed that there are 8 great tangible benefits of implementing the continuous practice of accountability:
    - ✓ *Trust*
    - ✓ *Communication*
    - ✓ *Ability to change*
    - ✓ *Drive for results*
    - ✓ *Honesty and integrity*
    - ✓ *Clear vision and direction*
    - ✓ *Problem-solving and technical expertise*
    - ✓ *Collaboration and the ability to resolve conflict*

When you have a healthy, God-enough esteem about yourself, you seek out anointed and authentic accountability partners. Moreover, you understand that having a divine circle of individuals who have a genuine heart to help you walk boldly in your enoughness is a collective blessing. Acts of accountability produce heavenly fruit that many people can eat and enjoy.

➢ **Acts of approachability:** I know, firsthand, that there is nothing worse than being connected to individuals and organizational leaders who are not approachable. The definition of approachable is *"being accessible, easy to meet or deal with; able to be met from a particular means or directions; free of strict barriers, unrealistic boundaries, and emotional and spiritual barricades."* Many times, people say they are approachable. However, they repeatedly dismiss, disrespect, ignore and exclude people.

They have a conditional and constrained philosophy of relating to others. They are truly walking in the spirit of error or deception. However, there is nothing confusing about being approachable. You either are or you are not. And people who are not approachable, struggle with being secure in their divine-given enoughness.

I recall serving under a boss who repeatedly told us that he had an open-door policy. He was erroneously persuading people that anyone could access him at any time for any reasons. However, his words were empty because his actions failed to align with them.

Despite his desperate measures to convince the staff of his approachable leadership, when you entered the office, there was red tape on the floor to signify that you were required to stop before you would proceed forward. In addition to the red tape on the floor, he had red-tape people who would aggressively and rudely bark at you if you did not adhere to the visual aids. Finally, when staff voiced their concerns about the contradictory open-door policy coupled with the disrespectful, dismissive, and derogatory public reprimands of selected employees on his leadership team, he had red-tape excuses for their behavior.

When you know you are competent, then approachability becomes a language that is apparent in word and action. Approachability goes far beyond being cordial, politically correct, and intentional. It is an action that proves you know, like, and walk in Godly confidence that empowers and equips others to operate in a healthy flow of positivity.

➤ **Acts of a bondservant:** In the New Testament times, a bondservant was viewed as one who ***willingly*** volunteered to permanently serve others. The motive of servanthood is for one reason only and that is of their ***commitment*** to Jesus. At no time does a bondservant have a desire to abandon their commitment to service.

The love language of being enough means that you act as a bondservant to the service of others. Now, I must correct some misconceptions. Being a bondservant does not mean you passively endure mistreatment of people because you have submitted yourself to servanthood. You can mistake your heart to serve as Jesus served by ignoring the actions of demonic abusers and assassins. That is not what being a bondservant means. Philippians 2:5-8 explains this concept with divine clarity:

"And consider the example that Jesus, the Anointed One, has set before us. Let his mindset become your motivation. He existed in the form of God, yet He gave no thought to seizing equality with God as His supreme prize. Instead, He emptied Himself of His outward glory by reducing Himself to the form of a lowly servant. He became human! He humbled Himself and became vulnerable, choosing to be revealed as a man and was obedient. He was a perfect example, even in His

death—a criminal's death by crucifixion!" (The Passion Translation.)

True bond-service entails that when you are attacked for the sake of Jesus, you respond, not react as He did. Jesus responded to mistreatment by living truth whether it was accepted or not. Jesus spoke truth to power in humility. Jesus poured Himself out so that in the midst of attacks, someone would be restored through how He stripped Himself of demanding His divine privileges. He released His rights. Since we were born and built God-enough, we should effortlessly demonstrate the love language of the acts of being a bondservant.

➢ **Quality of life that produces good fruit**—Fruit is the product of a seed-bearing plant that when it is ready for consumption, it is ripe, sweet, and has healthy nutritional substance. A life whose quality bears good fruit is one that has grown and completed the maturation process. It then can be harvested in the right season to be presented for its purpose of being consumed.

Colossians 1:10-11 in The Passion Translation explains, *"that you would walk in the ways of true righteousness, pleasing God in every good thing you do. Then you'll become fruit-bearing branches, yielding to*

His life, and maturing in the rich experience of knowing God in His fullness! And we pray that you would be energized with all His explosive power from the realm of His magnificent glory, filling you with great hope."

When you are walking in your God-enough lifestyle, the quality of your life produces fruit that people do not regret consuming. It is a righteous, healthy ingestion instead of a derogatory, hurtful infection. If you are demonstrating the purity of your enoughness, when people engage with you, there is a sweet savor that sustains them in the fullness of God. That fullness fuels a heavenly explosion of power, glory, and hope for you and those who interact with you.

➤ **Words of affirmation and inclusion**—The words we say to people can encourage or contaminate them. They can build or break an individual's spirit. Words can heal or kill. That is why Proverbs 18:21 proclaims, *"Words kill, words give life; they're either poison or fruit—you choose,"* (The Message Translation).

Words of affirmation offer emotional support and encouragement. They must not be used as a vehicle of flattery for selfish motives. Nor should they be the core of a sinister plot of deceptive destruction to eventually manipulate, malign, or misuse people.

On the contrary, words of affirmation must be spoken from a place of truth. They should always have a positive pronouncement over your life and endeavors. Words of affirmation ought to compel you to produce and prosper in your God-ordained purpose.

In that same vein of affirmation, your words need to promote inclusion. As you speak, people should feel a sense of becoming and belonging. Words of inclusion create a harmonious connection that makes others feel that you authentically want to develop a healthy connection for suitable socialization. Any words that are not affirming or inclusive, even in the midst of conflict, do not promote a love language of knowing that you are born and built God-enough.

The 3-Chord Strand of Loving Your Enoughness

Never forget that the "Yes, I Am Enough" message is rooted in Genesis 1:26-29. We are born God-enough because we were created in His image. We are built God-enough for He blessed us and instructed us to be fruitful, multiply, replenish the earth, and subdue it.

Finally, our Father commanded that we walk boldly in our enoughness. He declared that we have dominion over things in the sea, air, livestock, the earth and every other living thing that moves on the earth. The Lord also blessed us with covenant access to every seed-bearing plant on the earth and every tree that has fruit with seeds. These two gifts would be both food (for our necessary energy) and nourishment (for endurance, sustainability, and strength).

In essence, God made us uniquely **tailored** to be a reflection of Him. The Lord appointed us as **trustees** over His sacred estate. Lastly, He **transcended** us beyond living just to receive the essentials to experiencing the exceeding and abundant blessings.

So, because of this 3-chord strand of sovereign authority that the Lord lavished on us, we can walk in unwavering assurance. We have a bold fortitude because we lack nothing as children of God. We are absolutely, positively **ENOUGH!** And that is something to love.

Let us close with this chapter's "Yes, I Am Enough to Live at the Next Level" prayer affirmation:

"Heavenly Father, I praise you right now for Your unconditional love. Your love is truth. Your love is respectful. Master Your love does not deceive, discount or dismiss who I am or what You have predestined me to be. Your love is pure, peaceful and prosperous. Your love is giving for John 3:16 says that, 'For God so loved the world, that He gave His only begotten Son, that whosoever believeth in Him should not perish but have everlasting life.' **I AM ENOUGH TO GIVE AND RECEIVE THE TYPE OF AGAPE LOVE THAT YOU POUR OUT!**

"Sweet Savior, I repent of reducing Your perfect love toward me. I repent of loving myself, others and You less than the quality of love that You supply me with every second of the day. God, forgive me for cheapening Your agape love to being exclusive, conditional and based on who people are, what they do for me and if they make me feel happy. That is not the foundation of the love you demonstrate. Romans 5:8 makes it clear by saying, 'But God commendeth His love toward us, in that, while we were yet sinners, Christ died for us.' **YES, I AM ENOUGH TO WALK IN A PURE GODLY LOVE THAT SEES BEYOND MY SINFUL ACTIONS, YET STILL LOVES ME!**

"Lord, I thank You because Your love casts out all fear as 1 John 4:18 proclaims. Hallelujah! Your love inspires a fruitful future, one of positive peace and one of the expectations as Jeremiah 29:11 states. Master, I am overjoyed that when I embrace the essence of what You model love to be, it results in empowering me to shift my self-defeating thoughts to thoughts of being not just a conqueror, but more than a conqueror. Romans 8:37, 'Nay, in all these things we are more than conquerors through Him that loved us.' **OH, YES, I AM ENOUGH BECAUSE I AM MORE THAN A CONQUEROR THROUGH YOUR LOVE!**

"Finally, I am eternally grateful for Your love transforming me day by day. As I accept Your love, I develop a healthy self-love lifestyle. One that allows me to walk in love and display the 5 languages of loving my enoughness. Through Your love, I demonstrate acts of accountability so that I can always be

transparent. *I engage in acts of approachability, become a bondservant, being deliberate to do whatever it takes to have a life that produces fruit and freely speaks words of affirmation and inclusion over myself and others. I want to be saturated and overflowing in Your love. Romans 8:39 declares that absolutely* **NOTHING** *can or will separate me from Your love.* ***I AM ENOUGH TO BE LOVED AND TO LOVE OTHERS THE EXACT WAY THAT YOU LOVE ME!*** *I seal this affirming prayer in the name of Jesus. Amen."*

NEXT-LEVEL IMPLEMENTATION

In this chapter, I highlighted the Five Languages of Loving Your Enoughness. Complete the table on the next page as your personal language assessment. Identify who you believe you communicate your language of love toward and who communicates it toward you.

Also, reflect on next-level strategies for expanding your language of loving your enoughness toward people who you are estranged from for whatever reason. Remember, God demonstrated His love toward us not when we were loveable, but while we were unloveable. If you are truly desiring next-level enoughness, you will have to implement the Romans 5:8 love blueprint.

Language of loving your enoughness	Who you communicate this language of love toward	Who communicates this language of love toward you	Who you are not communicating this language of love toward due to a strain or rip in the relationship	Strategies you will implement to begin the process of healing the strained relationship to display the Romans 5:8 blueprint of communicating your language of love
Acts of accountability				
Acts of approachability				
Acts of a bondservant				
Quality of life that produces good fruit				
Words of affirmation and inclusion				

CHAPTER 4

Living Your Enoughness

"Every next level will demand a different version of you."
— www.livelifehappy.com

"Nearly all men can stand adversity, but if you want to test a man's character, give him power."
— Abraham Lincoln

"*Good is the enemy of great.*" These six future-shifting words begin the first chapter of the #1 *New York Times* Bestselling book by Jim Collins, *Good to Great: Why Some Companies Make the Leap and Others Don't.* The primary message of this literary phenomena is that the companies that jumped from being mediocre to magnificent had leaders operating at Level 5 leadership.

Collins explains in the book that Level 5 leadership in the executive hierarchy of capabilities builds sustainable greatness through the *"paradoxical blend of personal humility and professional will."* When leaders have an effortless flow at this level, they have conquered the craving to feed their ego. These secure leaders go against the grain by not performing out of a need for selfish accomplishments or accolades.

On the contrary, Level 5 leaders have mastered God's formula for universal impact—intentionality, humility, and fearlessness. These people live at the next level of their enoughness. They are driven by manifesting collective greatness instead of individual success.

Just like great companies, next-level living demands that you make next-level leaps toward greatness. You cannot be satisfied with going to higher levels by breaking the backs and spirits of people within your circles who help you. Level 5 individuals refuse to adopt that Yertle the Turtle spirit which compels them to crave selfish ambition so much that they use, abuse, manipulate, demand, and dictate how people help them.

"Yes, I Am Enough" minded people execute a vision. The goal of the God-enough visionary is to create an atmosphere of universal prosperity through encouraging, equipping and educating. Next-level mindsets require receiving and living truth in a transparent manner.

As I constantly embody and evolve into my own next-level enoughness, I strive to live at a Level 5. This invites a repeated stripping away of all things contrary to Genesis 1:26-29. The Lord opens my eyes to the myths that mire my motivation. He enlightens me to those who have ulterior motives of maligning my mind, emotions, and soul under the mask of manipulation and control. But most importantly, any misinformation and miseducation that I have knowingly and unknowingly accepted, God immediately exposes. Hebrews 12:1 instructs believers to *"let us lay aside every weight and the sin which doth so easily beset us, and let us run with patience the race that is set before us."* Exposure eventually produces a taste for walking in an awakened state. Being woke creates a thirst for more truth. That thirst for truth liberates us to eliminate more error so that elevation to the next level can occur.

The Miseducation of the 3 D's for Living in Your Enoughness

There is a supernatural system for authentically living in your enoughness. It is found in three dimensions- decreeing, declaring and demonstrating. However, there is a severe superficiality that is saturating our society. As a result of this, many individuals become excited about hearing certain news without comprehending the entire context of the news.

In the same manner, Christians follow suit oftentimes foregoing correctness because of the charismatic delivery. This is very true when it pertains to the biblical concepts of decreeing and declaring. Nevertheless, there is a specific conditional divine flow that you must comprehend when discussing the biblical philosophy of decreeing and declaring it.

A decree is the Lord's foreordaining will of something to occur in your life. You can trust whatever God decrees. Whether you like what He decrees or not, God never ever reneges on His word. If the Lord said it, it will surely and absolutely come to pass. You can stand flat-footed on Yahweh's heavenly issuance over your life.

Have you ever noticed that people have a certain elevated confidence, boldness and swagger when they are assured of something? A decree from the Most High is more valuable than money. It is filled with interest and profitability that yields supernatural dividends for all. Again, if God said it, it will surely come to pass.

Being a bonafide daddy's girl, I trusted everything my father told me. Even on the rare occasions that I had doubt, my daddy would always say to me, "Tee, have I ever steered you wrong? I am your daddy. My job is to provide and take care of you." And that would always shift my wavering faith.

People will tell you that I was that girl who was infamous for saying, "But my daddy said this or that." If someone contradicted my fathers' advice, it would not penetrate me because I trusted my daddy's dialogue. As a result of my father's power talks, eventually my own talk had power. My daddy empowered me to know, say and believe that I was enough many years before I would even think about writing the Yes, I Am Enough series books.

That is what happens when someone has proven that they want you to flourish in faith and favor. Their decree ignites you to make declarations that push you towards action. However, let me warn you. Beware when you declare! Divine and holy confident declarations tend to become a magnet for spiritual assassins.

Please remember, spiritual assassins can be operating out of demonic intention or unknown error. People respond to people from the level of their own self-perception. But whatever the case, spiritual assassins come to destroy the following areas. They attack your:

- **Peace**
- **Perspective**
- **Position in the relationships you have**
- **Patience**
- **Progress**
- **Purpose**

You will experience a great awakening when you become intentional about living at the next level. As I stated earlier, this type of holy confident living attracts demonic assassins. The most common demonic attack strategy is mind manipulation.

Mind manipulators are masters at trying to convince you to view yourself as less than who God has called you to be. Spiritual spinsters of this type will use the fallacy that your confidence is offensive to other Christians. They will dispense demonic advice for you to tone down who you are so that others can feel normal around you.

But the devil is a bald-faced ugly liar! You are born and built God **ENOUGH**! You shall not diminish your divine personhood to appease the anxiety of others. You confidently walking in your next level of enoughness will be abnormal and uncomfortable to others.

And you must be comfortable with making others feel uncomfortable when you are walking in the spirit of Jesus. The bible says that you are going to be strange to others who do not understand your royal lineage. *"But ye are a chosen generation, a royal priesthood, a holy nation a PECULIAR people; that ye should shew forth the praises of Him who hath called you out of darkness into His marvelous light,"* 1 Peter 2:9 King James Version.

Sadly, most of us will notice that we have passively allowed other people's abnormal perceptions of who we are and how we should live to birth doubt within us. What was once normal to us and working in our favor, becomes abnormal in our eyes when we have internalized the strange advice of others. You must be careful. Even those close to us who we respect highly will mistakenly miseducate us from the core of their own insecurities.

They do this because witnessing something different from what they are not used to seeing is abnormal to them. This type of abnormal is uncomfortable. So to relieve their feelings of uncomfortable abnormalcy when they are in your presence, they will continue to persuade you to believe that there is something abnormal about you. Your ways of being, thinking, and living are weird and unacceptable.

However, remember that your God-enoughness is always strange to insecure individuals. The advice they give you will be deceitful. It slowly shifts you from God's truth to man's version of truth. But please understand, your next level of living requires a transformation of your miseducation.

During an interview on my radio show *Real Talk With Tanya White,* Dallas Restore2Fitness Founder and Owner, Shonda Amie Dombrowsky shared that when she was molested at a young age it negatively impacted her. She explained that in the middle of all the mess around her, she had normalized the dysfunction. When you are living below your God-given authority, what is normal seems abnormal and what is abnormal seems normal.

Nevertheless, when you have reached your enough is enough point, you will dare to do something different. When I asked Shonda what she did to no longer normalize the dysfunction, she shared three triumphant tips. She stated that she shifted from allowing her pain to press down her enoughness when she:

- **TRACED It!**
- **FACED It!**
- **ERASED It!**

Dysfunction needs to be demolished in your life. Trace the origin of it. Face the hurt of it. And erase the negative and stifling effects of it.

Realize, that as you decree and declare what God has designed for you, it fuels you to discipline yourself. Discipline develops your dedication. Dedication births demonstration. It is the demonstration which expands your confidence in loving, living and sharing your enoughness.

Refuse to allow people's abnormal to become your new normal. Renounce every spirit that has spoken what is contradictory to God's declaration of you. Remember to decree, declare and to demonstrate that **YES, I AM ENOUGH!** Even in the face of those who may be uncomfortable around you because they are comfortable in their own insecurities declare **YES, I AM ENOUGH!** No excuses! No explanations! No compromises!

Let us close with our prayer affirmation:

"Precious Lord, I understand that my words bring death or life…hurt and hope…deceit or determination. I will remember that You, God, are my model of the power I have within me to change situations. Genesis 1:1 reminds me that one word from You can create life from the lifeless. God, I have been allowing my life to become lifeless for the mere fact that I have been living beneath my enoughness. But from this day on, I continuously decree and declare that YES, I AM ENOUGH!

"Master, forgive me for willingly accepting the miseducation of others. I repent of allowing other people who feel insecure, inferior, and inadequate to be an influential force of fake and

false motives. Lord, 1 Corinthians 15:33 speaks this powerful truth, 'So stop fooling yourselves! Evil companions will corrupt good morals and character.' Forgive me for being a fool toward myself. Immediately sever emotional soul ties from those who are bad company. I will do my part as you cut the ties by not spending quality time hanging out with people who are conscious or subconscious spiritual assassins. I will invest my time honing my purpose. **YES, I AM ENOUGH TO LIVE AT THE NEXT LEVEL! YES, I AM ENOUGH TO DECREE WHAT YOU DECREE! YES, I AM ENOUGH TO DECLARE WHAT YOU DECLARE! AND YES, I AM ENOUGH TO DEMONSTRATE THE HOLY EVIDENCE OF WHAT YOU WANT TO MANIFEST!** *In the name of Jesus. Amen."*

NEXT-LEVEL IMPLEMENTATION

In this chapter, I discussed what spiritual assassins are and how they come to destroy your:
- **Peace**
- **Perspective**
- **Position in the relationships you have**
- **Patience**
- **Progress**
- **Purpose**

Using the table on the following page, your assignment is to identify one spiritual assassin who has infiltrated your life whether they are in your past or present. Please remember, spiritual assassins can be operating out of demonic intention or unknown error. People respond to people from the level of their own self-perception.

Be specific as to how they worked to destroy the six things listed above. Also, explain the illusion that was birthed from this assassination attempt. Find a scripture for each category that will annihilate the illusions they created in your life. I suggest you repeat this exercise at least seven times to free yourself to walk even more boldly in your God-enoughness.

Name of spiritual assassin	How was this area attempted to be destroyed?	What illusion was created from this connection?	Scripture to annihilate the created illusion
Peace			
Perspective			
Position in relationships			
Patience			
Progress			
Purpose			

CHAPTER 5

Sharing Your Enoughness

> *"Happiness is not so much in having as in sharing. We make a living by what we get. But we make a life by what we give."*
> — Norman MacEwan

Next-level living brings next-level awareness. It is not about being focused on mediocre satisfaction with what you decree and declare. On the contrary, next-level living is about what you share with others.

In the previous chapter, I encouraged you to beware what you declare because of the demonic attacks. Now, I will suggest that you beware what you share. Not because of any demonic attacks. However, as you transparently share a piece of who you are, your influence impacts people near and far.

With my consulting clients, I discuss the importance of branding. Since 2005, my philosophy has been that branding is not what you do. Your brand is who you are. If you are promoting information about a brand that you are really not living, people will know.

Falsely developing a public brand that contradicts your private lifestyle will quickly compel people to know you, but not like or trust you. So, in essence, what you share becomes what others will declare. That is why I say beware what you share.

Next-level maturation in knowing that you are God-enough dictates how you share your enoughness. Your attitude shifts because you know that your approval, acceptance, and authorization comes from our Father in Heaven. Having God's seal of approval is what matters most.

Sharing yourself fuels your God-confidence. It has five life benefits, according to an article by Cynthia Kane via https://everydayfeminism.com:

- **Sharing makes you feel good:** Kane writes that *"when people share, their brains release the hormone oxytocin, sometimes called the 'feel good' or 'cuddle' hormone, which relieves stress."*

- **Sharing makes you grateful:** *"In the book, The Myths of Happiness, Sonja Lyubomirsky points out that "people who regularly practice appreciation or gratitude— who, for example, 'count their blessings' once a week over the course of one to twelve consecutive weeks— become reliably happier and healthier."*

➢ **Sharing increases trust:** Kane explains, "*Sharing gives us the opportunity to shed some of our suspicions of people. It's a great way to extinguish our doubt about what's good in the world.*" As you gratefully share and have an exuberate energy, people will focus more on what you have to say and how you say it. They listen with the intent to learn instead of with the intent to respond. As a result, they will discover the commonalities they have with you. Those commonalities inspire them to persevere to achieve the manner of God-confidence that you have. Ultimately, your transparency to share develops a trust within them to reciprocate the sharing.

➢ **Sharing makes life real:** Authentic sharing, with the goal to inspire and motivate instead of boast and discriminate, makes life genuine. However, do not be tripped up by people who reject your heart to share. Do not be discouraged by those who misinterpret or malign your willingness to share your God-competence.

Remember, we are living in a world plagued by pseudoism, as I explained in Chapter 2. People are believing the fake as real and rejecting what's real because they think it is fake. But when you are loving and living at the next level of your enoughness, your sharing will become an unstoppable part of your life.

Sharing Your Enoughness

You will be exactly like the leper in Mark 1:40-45 that Jesus healed and told not to tell anyone until he arrived home. But because the leper was extremely grateful, delivered, and set free from years of bondage, he just could not contain his good news. The Bible details that as the leper left, he just could not keep his deliverance to himself.

He told everyone about what Jesus did for him and how he was restored. Sharing steeped in recognizing that you were once bound, once ostracized, maligned and mistreated ignites such an infectious public demonstration that people notice your genuine transforamtion. You become grateful because you know that you are God-**ENOUGH!**

> ➢ **Sharing means you are not alone:** Kane continues to enlighten readers in the article by explaining, "*Thinking we can live life without letting others have or use a part of what belongs to us can make us feel isolated, almost like no one in the world cares or could understand. But when we share with others, what we learn is that we're actually creating more joy, gratitude, trust, and community— not only for ourselves, but also for the world.*"

As I grow in the next levels of enoughness, my growth and transformation inspire me to empower others. The joy and awareness that I now have delivers me from self-imposed isolations and social manipulations. I am experiencing a freedom unlike I have never known possible. So, my sharing becomes ingrained in my lifestyle.

However, I have noticed that impactful sharing is not just what you say. Sharing also is a demonstration of what you do. When you are walking in a Godly boldness, your sharing produces what I have pinned the **C-I-A** enoughness indicators. The impact of your sharing is demonstrated through these twelve principles of assurance in your ability and capability. Let us explore these **C-I-A** principles.

Character, Clarity, Connections, and Conflict-Resolution

Character controls everything in your life. Your character can either contribute to your success or cost you Godsent support. Some divine connections that were designed to elevate you to the never-been-seen or heard-of-before levels become disconnections due to your character bloopers.

You can research limitless stories of people whose negative, moral, and mental qualities messed up their miracles in the making. Once in influential places of universal significance or on the runway to flying off to higher places, people with corrupt character credentials issue their own cease and desist orders that force all of God's activities of ascension to stop.

Lack of character also broods a lack of clarity or vision. I will use the words *clarity* and *vision* interchangeably. Visionless people are not secure in who they are because they are committed to masking themselves. They get bitten by the "I'm so busy" bug of empty daily routines as a defense mechanism of avoiding operating in clarity. Individuals who are willingly and easily distracted by every person, proposition and easy pathways to superficial prosperity send red flags that scream, **"NO, I AM NOT ENOUGH!"**

I have experiences of how a person of vision working with a person with limited or no vision frustrates their entire community. There is absolutely nothing worse than being under a leader—whether in your home, on your job, in your church, or even in your government—who deliberately chooses to be visionless. People with vision inadvertently birth individual and collective victory. In the same manner, people who are void of vision cultivate a culture of insecurity, inferiority, and inadequacy.

People with clarity about who they are and where they are going, communicate it without even saying a word. There is a saying, *"The proof is in the pudding."* When you believe you are enough, vision becomes necessary. Leadership guru John Maxwell once quoted, *"Good leaders must communicate vision clearly, creatively, and continually. However, the vision does not come alive until the leader models it."*

That is what next-level sharing of your enoughness is about. You move from merely talking about who you are and what you are going to achieve to modeling it. Clarity compels you to confidently move to manifest your talk into your walk.

Character and clarity impact who you connect with as well. Let me repeat what my wonderful daddy, Joe White, Sr.

imparted into us growing us. *"If you want to be a dummy then go ahead and hang around dummies. But if you want to be smart, then you must hang around smart people."* Point. Blank. Period!

People who want to love, live, and share that they are God-enough are intentional about connecting with like-minded people. "No, I Am Not Enough" people innately align with other "No, I Am Not Enough" people. This collective security in their own insecurity, inadequacy, and inferiority creates a barrage of delusional strongholds.

Delusional strongholds are thoughts that are fortified by maintaining fixed, false, and unrealistic beliefs even when confronted with facts. They develop killer distractions. They deceive you from the truth, seduce you to twist God's Word and standards. Delusional strongholds will have you engaging in destructive behaviors, experiencing extreme emotional, spiritual, and financial suffering, yet acting and telling people that you are in the best season of your life.

Delusional strongholds have you drawn to connections that are not covenant relations but ones of convenience. These entanglements are with people who cosign your chaos instead of holding you accountable to what is pure, right, and acceptable in the loving eyes of the Lord. As a result, "No, I Am Not Enough" relationships do not cultivate effective conflict resolution. On the contrary, conflict is avoided. In addition, you begin a game of playing the victim, blaming others, and severing ties because you refuse to heal.

But when you know that you are God's reflection and His child, your character mirrors His character. Mirroring the Lord's character creates clarity in your life. A clear vision helps you to be careful about your inner circle connections.

In addition, Godly character and clarity transform your perspective concerning your inner circle connections. Your associations become those iron-sharpening people who challenge and coach you to your next level. And then you know that conflict is not a negative attribute of relationships. In fact, conflict resolution becomes your necessary avenue of metamorphic portions, which positively pressures you to conduct a serious self-assessment. Being confident in your next-level enoughness allows you to handle conflict resolution with grace and gratitude instead of begrudgingly.

Integrity, Intercession, Innovation, and Instruction

In this world of pseudoism, integrity is trying to slowly become extinct, which is why the Yes, I Am Enough movement is such a daily burden for me to embody, love, live, and share. It is through having this internal consistency and lack of internal delusion that people evolve into their optimal enoughness.

It is through being intentional about living in integrity that a sense of trust returns in our homes, churches, and the world. It is in this state of being whole and uncompromisingly undivided that you have the mind to move in your destiny. Integrity is the energizer that ignites next-level internal security. It also prompts others influenced by you to check their integrity thermometer as well.

Next, is the power of intercession that demonstrates evidence in your life. Now, when we automatically think about intercession, we visualize someone on their knees, bombarding heaven in prayer. However, living at an elevated level of enoughness expands our perspective of intercession.

Apostle Matthew Stevenson, Pastor and Founder of the All Nations Worship Assembly Chicago, once quoted in a sermon that intercession means to "intervene." It means to step in between two parties to bring about change. So, in that vein of understanding, intercession is more than just praying. It is participating in leveraging your resources to share with others to create opportunities that can help propel them to the next level of living.

Next, is the concept of innovation. Innovation is oftentimes limited to what businesses should be doing. But, when we are walking securely in who we are, our lives become instruments of innovation. We should have new ideas about how to produce our divine purpose. Innovation is a product of strategic and successful problem solving of ineffective or outdated processes. As you walk in the "Yes, I Am Enough" next-level lifestyle, you are constantly evaluating your life, your systems of thinking, living and being as well as birthing better solutions.

Pastor Josh Hart of All Nations Worship Assembly of Louisville, preached in a sermon entitled "The Spirit of

Embodying Your Enoughness

- **M**ove in Your Enoughness Confidently!—This is the last piece of the **S.T.E.A.M.** puzzle. Moving in the confidence of knowing you are enough is an act of faith. And faith without works is dead, is what James 2:17 tells us.

  When you are confident, you have an unwavering feeling of firm trust in the truth about something. You are competent as a result of a strongly held belief or theory. Embodying your enoughness shows that you live, move, and breathe that you are equipped with absolutely everything you need.

  Develop Muhammad Ali's philosophy when moving confidently in who you are. You will float like a butterfly. Sting the devil as well as his minions like a bee. Moving in the momentum of "Yes, I Am Enough" will **M**anifest **O**pportunities and **V**ictories that will **E**levate you to your next level.

In closing, remember that you are not alone in your battle to embody your enoughness. I am writing this book because I am a recovering "No, I'm Not Enough" addict. Just like alcohol, food, and drugs, you can escape your reality by digesting the unhealthy concept that you are not good enough, capable enough, and any other enoughisms you battle. But the "No, I Am Not Enough" addiction will lead you to self-destruction.

So, before we move to the next chapter, let me help you to deliver yourself by boldly declaring this chapter's "Yes, I

Am Enough to Live at the Next Level" prayer affirmation. This will give you extra **S.T.E.A.M.** to embody the tangible evidence that you are **ENOUGH!**

"Dear Lord, I admit that I have created my own powerlessness by not understanding my God-given enoughness. I have created unnecessary chaos, confusion, and stagnation because I believed that lie that I was lacking something. **BUT I LACK NOTHING! YES, I AM ENOUGH!**

Genesis 1:26-27 is the foundation of everything I am. First, God, You created me in Your divine image. With being made in the image of the Master of Creation, I automatically am endowed with divine rulership over the fish in the sea and the birds in the sky, over the livestock and all the wild animals, and over all the creatures that move along the ground. **AGAIN, I LACK NOTHING! YES, I AM ENOUGH!**

I declare that I am blessed, bountiful, and built to bear even more fruit according to Genesis 1:28-29. Jehovah Jireh, You blessed me and prophetically declared that I be fruitful and increase in number; fill the earth and subdue it. Rule over the fish in the sea and the birds in the sky and over every living creature that moves on the ground. Then, as the culmination of Your divine creation, Lord, You gave me every seed-bearing plant on the face of the whole earth and every tree that has fruit with seed in it. **SO, I LACK NOTHING! YES, I AM ENOUGH BECAUSE I WAS BORN GOD-ENOUGH! I WAS BUILT GOD-ENOUGH! I WAS BLESSED GOD-ENOUGH! YES, I AM ENOUGH!"** *In Jesus' mighty and matchless name. Amen."*

Religion," that when people and organizations are more committed to their practices, they never make progress. "No, I Am Not Enough" individuals get happy about speaking about their plans to progress in order to receive the "rah-rah" from others. On the other hand, "Yes, I Am Enough" soldiers get moving and implement strategic, sustainable, and innovative plans to manifest results.

Finally, the last installment of the "I" component in the **C-I-A** principle is instruction. There is an old proverb that says, *"When the student is ready, the teacher will appear."* Next-level God-confidence craves authentic instruction. Knowledge is definitely power. When you know better, you can live better.

Nancy Merz Nordstrom wrote in her article "Top 10 Benefits of Lifelong Learning" on https://www.selfgrowth.com that people should expect rewards from being open to instruction. Some benefits of learning ranked from numbers 10 to 1 include:

10. Lifelong learning helps us fully develop natural abilities.
9. Lifelong learning opens the mind.
8. Lifelong learning creates a curious, hungry mind.
7. Lifelong learning increases our wisdom.
6. Lifelong learning makes the world a better place.
5. Lifelong learning helps us adapt to change.

4. Lifelong learning helps us find meaning in our lives.
3. Lifelong learning keeps us involved as active contributors to society.
2. Lifelong learning helps us make new friends and establish valuable relationships.
1. Lifelong learning leads to an enriching life of self-fulfillment.

Consistently ingesting correct teaching that gives hope, healing, and guidance makes your enoughness bubble over like a volcano about to erupt. Be courageous enough to move away from people, places, and institutions that have stopped teaching. In addition, beware of instruction that has become exclusive and practices elitism. This stifles your freedom to share.

Remember, what you learn shapes how you live. Apostle Matthew Stevenson once encouraged his social media family with these words, *"The RIGHT CHURCH matters. Your life is the byproduct of the teaching you're submitted to. Things may not be manifesting in your life because it's not being revealed in your church. Doctrine determines life. If your teaching is poor, so are you"* It is not enough to have instruction from anywhere or anyone. When you are built God-enough you must have competent teaching based in truth, faith, and tangible evidence of empowerment in the instructor's own life.

Attitude, Authenticity, Acceptability, and Advisability

I ran across an anonymous quote that proclaimed, *"Your attitude is like a price tag. It shows how valuable you are."* In my "No, I Am Not Enough" days, I had the worst attitude. I would tell people off in a split second when I felt disrespected, dismissed, or devalued. You know that as a writer, I am never at a loss for words…some very choice words at that.

I cringe thinking about how my attitude tore people down and made them feel less than. I pushed them away because of my passive aggressive anger. I always debated people deliberately as a defense mechanism all because I felt extremely inadequate in everything.

Actually, my attitude could not completely change until I unleashed my authentic self. Authenticity shifts and lifts your attitude toward yourself and toward others. Wearing masks is much harder work than being your true self.

Furthermore, being the true you transforms your attitude from negative to positive. Your positive attitude emits energy that allows you to accept the good, bad, and the ugly of who you are. It does the same with your perspective toward other people. Acceptability opens once-closed-off hearts and minds to embrace the newness of feeling self-assured.

The last principle is advisability. A foul attitude forms from inauthentic personhood. Not being genuine creates an environment of exclusivity. Your environment of only surrounding yourself with people you feel comfortable around because they refuse to challenge you makes receiving advice from others impossible. Check your attitude, add your authenticity, and multiply your acceptability. Then you can embrace wisdom from experienced and sound advisability.

Revelation 12:11 is clear that we are overcomers not only by the blood that Jesus shed for us, but by the word of our testimony. **YES, I AM ENOUGH** are four words of triumph that prompts you to share it with everyone you encounter. Like the leper mentioned in Mark 1:40-45, as a result of being made whole and finally recognizing that you are enough, you will not be able to keep that good news to yourself. Nor should you. You will say and show everyone you encounter that **YES, I AM ENOUGH!**

Now, let us read our prayer affirmation:

"Gracious and merciful Father, I am in awe of how You continuously keep forgiving me when I can do things that in human eyes can seem unforgivable. I am grateful for Your grace even though I sometimes do not extend it to others. Thank You for always sharing Yourself with me. Thank You for speaking to me when I ignore others and sometimes close my ears to what You have to say. As your word says in Deuteronomy 31:8, 'The LORD himself goes before you and will be with you; he will never leave you nor forsake you. Do not be afraid; do not be discouraged.' **YES, I AM ENOUGH TO KNOW THAT YOU LOVE ME AND THAT YOU WILL NEVER LEAVE NOR FORSAKE ME!**

Sharing Your Enoughness

"Lord, thank You for being the utmost example of what sharing is. You lavishly give me all things…my needs and wants. Your word is true in Matthew 6:33 that says that if I seek first the Kingdom of God, then all things will be added unto me. Adding character, contentment, authenticity, and innovation are just a few components that have freed me to be unashamedly me. **YES, I AM ENOUGH TO DARE TO SUBMIT TO AND TO SHARE THE REAL ME!**

"Finally, God, I pray that I stay in the vein of victory. Victory in my mind. Victory in my spirit and soul. Victory in all things. When You are exalted, I know the devil really is defeated. And I have the victory. It is in my victory that I will be excited and motivated to share the good news with others. I will demonstrate that I am confident in who You created me to be by my lifestyle. People will see tangible evidence of the blessings of walking in my God-enoughness. As Acts 17:28 reminds me, 'For in Him we live and move and have our being.' **YES, I AM ENOUGH TO SHARE MY LIFE WITH OTHERS!** It is in the redeeming and reconciling name of Jesus that I pray. Amen."

NEXT-LEVEL IMPLEMENTATION

In this chapter, I revealed the concept of **delusional strongholds.** In the space below, answer the following questions:

1) Identify the delusional strongholds that have become a barrier to living boldly in your God-confidence.

_____
_____
_____
_____
_____
_____

2) Reflect on the origin of these strongholds. Determine where you were physically, emotionally and spiritually. Identify who was in your circle of influence.

_____
_____
_____
_____
_____

Sharing Your Enoughness

3) Explain how you are breaking or have broken those delusional strongholds.

_____
_____
_____
_____
_____
_____
_____
_____

CLOSING

YES, I AM ENOUGH!
From the Next Level to Being Magnetically Phenomenal

"Creating the next level of walking in your enoughness, requires next level of thinking that is deeper and intentional. The next level of deeper thinking about your enoughness requires the next level of vision casting for your life. The next level of vision casting requires the next level of you listening to the Lord and to wise people who are living with moral, ethical and spiritual integrity." — Tanya White

- *Jesus Christ*
- *Oprah Winfrey*
- *Magic Johnson*
- *Mother Teresa*
- *Maya Angelou*
- *Iyanla Vanzant*
- *Billy Graham*
- *Dr. Martin Luther and Coretta Scott King*
- *President Barack and First Lady Michelle Obama*

Closing

The above list entails just a few individuals who are what I have pinned as being **Magnetically Phenomenal** in my book. In my first *Yes, I Am Enough* installment, I discussed that being magnetically phenomenal is having that God-confidence that becomes contagious to everyone. They may not know exactly why they are drawn to you, but it is because of God's spirit working in through and around you.

First Lady Michelle Obama quoted at the life celebration of Dr. Maya Angelo that, *"Dr. Angelou didn't just want to be phenomenal by herself. She wanted all of us to be phenomenal, so she took us under her wing and taught us."* Being magnetically phenomenal is unselfishly mentoring others with the essential tools they need to succeed. That is how all of these people on my list lived and are living today. Jesus Christ is the best example of them all.

When you are determined to become magnetically phenomenal like the Lord, you will be committed and consecrated to certain ways of living. God will reveal to you that being magnetically phenomenal like Him is not an act to do in order to obtain something. On the contrary, it is a process of continuously becoming a blessing to God and yourself, as well as others.

I am a witness that embracing my magnetic phenomenalism is a journey. A journey that only God and myself truly understand. When the Lord deposited this philosophy in my spirit, it blew my mind. I reflected on this divine new theory of living. I internalized the depth of transformation that it would bring.

I studied other models who I believed were magnetically phenomenal. Their journeys were intriguing. I learned that people who had this trait really did not know it.

Like those I admired, God showed me that this new concept of being magnetically phenomenal was a byproduct of me walking in the fullness of my enoughness. So, I started saying it. I wrote about it. I was humbly excited about being and encouraging others to be magnetically phenomenal. Yes, I was enough to decree and declare my magnetic phenomenalism.

But when I moved past speaking and studying God's divine revelation to actually living it with intentionality and consistency, I attracted more than I bargained for. Of course, there were people who understood and were elated to embrace being magnetically phenomenal themselves. However, the naysayers and negative Nathans and Negative Nancys around me came to challenge and curtail me from saying that I was magnetically phenomenal. One minister, operating under the mask of his own insecurity, actually tried to use his position to persuade me not to say that I was magnetically phenomenal. He said that was offensive to others.

I admit I was livid. I was angry. I was hurt. I was confused. Why would someone I thought that I was growing

Closing

to respect deflect me from embodying my divine freedom? It was simple. They were advising me from their own limited view of themselves. As I have stated before, people who do not believe that they are enough will always debate your enoughness.

Growing stronger in your sanctified security will reveal the truth and deceptive motives of people. Whether the deception is intentional or unintentional the impact is the same. You will have to work to annihilate that illusion that was birthed through a word curse spoken to you.

In closing, to become magnetically phenomenal, you must:

Meditate on God's Word so it becomes your daily soul food.

Appreciate people both privately and publicly.

Get a growth-mindset that is ingrained in all endeavors.

Never view others as a threat but as an indispensable treasure you can inspire and learn from.

Enthusiastically and infectiously release positive energy that shifts atmospheres and situations.

Take the time to nurture your Godsent connections without selfish motives.

Inspect and correct negative attitudes, actions, and associations.

Courageously live in the character of God. It is the cornerstone of your attraction.

By now, I pray that you have truly comprehended that these four words: **YES, I AM ENOUGH** are powerful to say. However, never stop at the point of only speaking these words. On the contrary, for you to produce tangible results in your life, you must continuously level up. *Yes, I Am Enough the Next Level* takes you on an ever-evolving journey. You will grow through these processes more than once.

Evolve into a greater understanding of your enoughness! Embody your enoughness! Love it! Live it! Share it! Make it a morning routine to look in the mirror before you start preparing for the day and after you spend time with the Lord and boldly tell yourself, **"YES, I AM ENOUGH! AND I'M LOVING, LIVING AND SHARING MY ENOUGHNESS WITH ALL I ENCOUNTER!"**

Now, shout this final prayer affirmation from the top of your lungs:

*"Our Father who is in heaven and on earth thank You for being my **ENOUGH** example so that I can walk in my enoughness. Thank You for having me on Your mind at the beginning of creation. Thank You for creating me in Your divine image. Thank You for blessing me to be fruitful and multiply the resources You entrusted me with on this earth. There are not enough words or time to say thank You. But I can show it every*

Closing

day and in every way by evolving and embodying that **YES, I AM ENOUGH!**

"Lord, I want to be **MAGNETICALLY PHENOMENAL** just like you, drawing people out of darkness, despair, defeat, discouragement, and demonic deception. I want my word and wonderful acts of love to be a magnet of phenomenal magnitude, changing lives for generations to come. As Philippians 4:13 proclaims 'I can do all things through Christ who strengthens me.' I can be strengthened to be **MAGNETICALLY PHENOMENAL** because **I AM ENOUGH IN YOU!**

"You are the Master **Magnet** who does **Phenomenal** things in those You draw to You by Your spirit. God, Your Word says in John 6:44 'If the Father who sent Me does not draw you, then there's no way you can come to Me.' Savior, Your Word declares in James 4:8 as I draw close to You, by washing my hands and purifying my heart, You will draw closer to me for my loyalty will not be divided between You and the world.

"Lord, in John 12:32 Jesus said that, 'If I be lifted up, I will draw all men unto me.' So, God, as I walk in my God-confidence, knowing that I lack nothing because I live in You, I can lift Jesus up in what I say and do. I will become a living epistle of Matthew 5:14-16, being that holy light, shining on the hilltop of life, allowing the good deeds you do through me to draw people to you so that they will glorify You! Oh, yes! I will become like You—**MAGNETICALLY PHENOMENAL! YES, I AM ENOUGH! YES, I WILL LOVE, LIVE,** and **SHARE MY**

ENOUGHNESS AT MY NEXT LEVEL OF LIVING! I seal this prayer of affirmation in the mighty, matchless, and delivering power of Jesus. Amen."

Closing

NEXT-LEVEL IMPLEMENTATION

For the next ten days, spend time focusing on reading one chapter from the Bible each morning. Journal three to five lessons learned from the chapter. Write a reflection, including how the scripture is speaking to your current situations and struggles. Finally, write a **YES, I AM ENOUGH** prayer of affirmation. After the ten days, repeat it. I promise you that you will feel ten times better.

REFERENCES
(as they appear in the book)

Marder, L. (2018, September 23). Mark Twain: His Life and His Humor. Retrieved from https://www.thoughtco.com/mark-twain-biography-4142835

Richmond-Davis, B. *Taking Off the Mask*. Kentucky

Burton, N. M.D. (2016, June 25). These Are the 7 Types of Love. Retrieved from https://www.psychologytoday.com/us/blog/hide-and-seek/201606/these-are-the-7-types-love

Business Dictionary, www.businessdictionary.com

Folkman. J. Retrieved from https://www.forbes.com/search/?q=joseph folkman#6aa95cf6279f

Kane, Cynthia. (2014, March 11). 5 Benefits of Sharing. Retrieved from https://everydayfeminism.com/2014/03/5-benefits-of-sharing/

Dr. Matthew Stevenson (2019, March 12, 2019) Retrieved from https://facebook.com/489060771160330/posts/2191065117626545

Pastor Josh Hart. Sermon *The Spirit of Religion*. March 10, 2019. All Nations Worship Assembly Louisville. 10 AM Service

www.ingramcontent.com/pod-product-compliance
Lightning Source LLC
Chambersburg PA
CBHW070133100426
42744CB00009B/1818